A FIRST for
EVERYTHING
journal

A FIRST for
EVERYTHING
journal

CHRONICLE BOOKS
SAN FRANCISCO

INTRODUCTION

Your first address. Your first love. Your first boss. Your first time sneaking out of the house. From love and friendship to work and play, our first experiences are the touchstones we continue to revisit throughout our lives. They help us define who we are as individuals and remind us where we came from, even as life rushes past. Before we know it, our firsts have blurred into seventeenths and somehow we've lost track of our beginnings.

This journal is your place to recall all your most important, not-so-important, as well as some of your craziest, firsts. Don't be shy—events that felt devastatingly embarrassing at the time often seem laughable in retrospect. And conversely, episodes that felt insignificant back then take on greater importance in hindsight. Only through jotting them down will you be able to tell the difference.

A First for Everything Journal is organized into eight categories. Each gives an opportunity to explore first milestones in different areas of your life, whether it's your first possessions, first experiences, first people, first places, or first favorite things. There's no right way to work through it—just see which entries inspire you. Flip through, skip around, and let your interests be your guide.

Most prompts include additional questions that may spur your memory further. Don't hold back if more memories spring to mind. Writing about your first road trip might make you remember the mixtape you listened to on the drive or the "quirky" motel that had only cold water. This is your journal. Feel free to write as much or as little as you like.

As you work your way through, take the opportunity to reflect on what your firsts have to say about you and how you've grown as an individual. How have your tastes evolved since your first favorites? How much did your first friendships and relationships influence those you have formed since? Looking deeper into your personal origins can uncover a wealth of insights and food for thought.

And while this journal can be an invaluable vehicle for self-discovery, keep in mind that it should also be fun! If you're not feeling a certain section, move on to another that sparks your imagination. The most important thing is to enjoy the experience, no matter where your journey of self-discovery leads.

After you've filled it in, you'll have a keepsake record of your life's origins, including everything from your first school to your first album to your first car. Make a mental note to revisit your entries weeks, months, or even years afterward. Some will feel embarrassing, some rewarding, and others will remind you of what you once deemed momentous. It's fascinating to reread what you wrote about and see what new memories pop up the second, third, or even tenth time around. You might even be inspired to continue jotting down new firsts as they unfold—after all, there's a first for everything.

FIRST THINGS

FIRST WORD:

FIRST CATCHPHRASE:

FIRST NICKNAME

NAME:

WHO GAVE IT TO YOU?

WHAT DID IT MEAN?

FIRST JOKE

JOKE:

WHERE DID YOU LEARN IT?

FIRST JOKE YOU MADE UP:

FIRST DOCTOR

NAME:

WERE YOU SCARED TO GO?

FIRST INJURY THAT
REQUIRED STITCHES

BODY PART:

HOW DID IT HAPPEN?

FIRST BROKEN BONE

BONE:

HOW DID YOU DO IT?

HOW LONG IT TOOK TO HEAL:

WHAT YOU WORE WHILE IT HEALED:

FIRST ALLERGY:

FIRST LOST TOOTH

HOW DID YOU LOSE IT?

AMOUNT LEFT BY TOOTH FAIRY.

FIRST MOTHER'S DAY
GIFT YOU GAVE:

FIRST FATHER'S DAY
GIFT YOU GAVE:

FIRST MEMORABLE BIRTHDAY PARTY

AGE:

CAKE:

LOCATION:

GUESTS:

MEMORABLE PRESENTS:

FIRST STUFFED ANIMAL

NAME:

SPECIES:

WHERE DID YOU GET IT?

FIRST PET

NAME:

SPECIES:

NOTABLE PERSONALITY TRAITS:

FIRST HAIRCUT YOU CHOSE FOR YOURSELF

AGE:

STYLE:

HOW DID IT TURN OUT?

FIRST BICYCLE

MAKE AND COLOR:

WHEN DID YOU LEARN TO RIDE?

WHO TAUGHT YOU?

FIRST CARPOOL

DRIVER:

RIDERS:

FIRST AIRPLANE RIDE

DESTINATION:

WERE YOU SCARED?

FIRST FAMILY CAR

MAKE AND MODEL:

YEAR:

COLOR:

FIRST BEDTIME

TIME:

WOULD YOU FIGHT TO STAY UP?

BEDTIME RITUALS:

FIRST SATURDAY MORNING RITUAL:

FIRST CHORE

DUTY:

HOW OFTEN DID YOU HAVE TO
DO IT?

FIRST ALLOWANCE

AMOUNT:

DAY RECEIVED:

PARENTAL CONDITIONS:

FIRST DREAMS

FIRST DREAM YOU REMEMBER:

_____

_____

_____

_____

FIRST RECURRING DREAM:

_____

_____

_____

_____

FIRST NIGHTMARE:

_____

_____

_____

_____

FIRST HOMEMADE INVENTION

NAME:

FUNCTION:

DID IT WORK?

FIRST LUCKY CHARM

CHARM:

WHERE DID YOU GET IT?

WHAT MADE YOU THINK IT WAS LUCKY?

FIRST MEMORABLE HALLOWEEN COSTUME

COSTUME:

WAS IT PURCHASED OR HOMEMADE?

FIRST MOVIES

FIRST MOVIE YOU REMEMBER WATCHING:

FIRST MOVIE YOU SAW IN A THEATER:

FIRST MOVIE THAT SCARED YOU:

FIRST MOVIE THAT MADE YOU CRY:

FIRST MOVIE YOU PURCHASED:

FIRST CANDY ADDICTION

CANDY:

WHERE YOU USUALLY PURCHASED IT:

WEEKLY CONSUMPTION:

FIRST CONTEST YOU ENTERED

NAME:

PRIZE:

DID YOU WIN?

FIRST VIDEO GAMES

CONSOLE:

GAMES YOU PLAYED:

WHO WOULD PLAY WITH YOU?

FIRST TEAM SPORT PLAYED

SPORT:

POSITION:

COACH:

TEAMMATES:

DID YOUR TEAM EVER WIN?

FIRST CLUB YOU JOINED

NAME:

MEMBERS:

PRIMARY ACTIVITIES:

FIRST CREATIVE WRITING PROJECT:

FIRST POEM YOU HAD TO RECITE FROM MEMORY

TITLE:

FORUM:

AUDIENCE:

FIRST FOREIGN LANGUAGE YOU STUDIED:

FIRST VOLUNTEER ACTIVITY

LOCATION:

DUTIES:

HOW LONG DID YOU DO IT FOR?

FIRST SCIENCE FAIR

PROJECT:

PARTNER(S):

GRADE:

FIRST REWARD FOR GOOD GRADES:

FIRST MUSICAL INSTRUMENT

INSTRUMENT:

DID YOU TAKE LESSONS?

SONG YOU PLAYED MOST:

FIRST MONEY-MAKING SCHEME

WHAT WAS IT?

AMOUNT MADE:

FIRST COLLECTION OF THINGS

ITEMS:

WHEN AND WHERE DID YOU ACQUIRE YOUR FIRST?

FIRST POSTER YOU
HUNG ON YOUR WALL:

FIRST PORTABLE
MUSIC PLAYER:

FIRST ALBUM YOU PURCHASED

TITLE:

ARTIST/BAND:

HOW YOU HEARD ABOUT IT:

WHERE YOU PURCHASED IT:

FIRST MIXTAPE MADE	FIRST MIXTAPE RECEIVED
FOR:	FROM:
WHEN:	WHEN:
TRACK LIST:	TRACK LIST:

FIRST COMPUTER

BRAND:

PRIMARY USE:

FIRST EMAIL ADDRESS:

FIRST CELL PHONE

MODEL:

PHONE NUMBER:

MONTHLY COST:

WHAT HAPPENED TO IT?

FIRST THING YOU LEARNED TO COOK

DISH:

WHEN WOULD YOU MAKE IT?

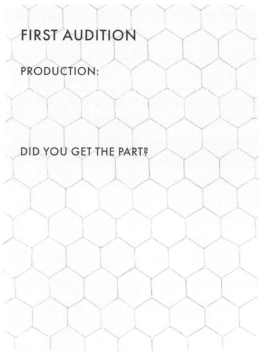

FIRST AUDITION

PRODUCTION:

DID YOU GET THE PART?

FIRST MAGAZINE SUBSCRIPTION:

FIRST PIECE OF CLOTHING YOU BEGGED TO GET

ARTICLE:

WHY DID YOU WANT IT SO MUCH?

FIRST FASHION BLUNDER:

FIRST PIECE OF JEWELRY OR ACCESSORY YOU WERE GIFTED:

FIRST CURFEW

TIME:

FIRST TIME YOU BROKE CURFEW:

FIRST THING STOLEN FROM YOU

ITEM:

WHO DO YOU THINK STOLE IT?

DID YOU EVER GET IT BACK?

FIRST PIERCING

LOCATION ON BODY:

WHAT DID THE JEWELRY LOOK LIKE?

DO YOU STILL HAVE IT?

FIRST CAR YOU DROVE

MODEL AND YEAR:

WAS IT YOURS?

WHO TAUGHT YOU TO DRIVE IT?

FIRST CAR YOU BOUGHT

MODEL AND YEAR:

HOW MUCH DID IT COST?

FIRST TICKET:

FIRST ACCIDENT:

FIRST BIG PURCHASE

ITEM:

HOW DID YOU EARN THE MONEY?

HOW LONG DID YOU HAVE TO SAVE?

FIRST JOB

POSITION: SALARY:

BOSS: WHAT WERE YOUR HOURS?

WAS THERE A DRESS CODE?

WHAT DID YOU SPEND YOUR FIRST PAYCHECK ON?

FIRST PIECE OF FURNITURE PURCHASED

ITEM:

WHERE DID YOU BUY IT?

COST:

FIRST FEELINGS

FIRST MEMORY:

FIRST THING YOU WANTED
TO BE WHEN YOU GREW UP

CHILDHOOD ASPIRATION:

WHAT GAVE YOU THE IDEA?

FIRST THING PEOPLE TEASED YOU ABOUT:

FIRST FEAR

WHAT WAS IT?

FIRST TIME YOU FELT IT:

HOW DID YOU OVERCOME IT?

FIRST EMBARRASSING MOMENT

WHAT HAPPENED?

WITNESSES:

DID YOU CRY?

FIRST OBSESSION

WHAT WAS IT?

HOW IT PASSED:

FIRST TIME YOU FELT LONELY:

FIRST TIME YOU REMEMBER CRYING

CIRCUMSTANCES:

FIRST TIME YOU CRIED IN FRONT OF A NON-FAMILY MEMBER:

FIRST EXPERIENCE WITH LOSS

WHAT HAPPENED?

HOW YOU COPED:

FIRST PET PEEVE

ANNOYING BEHAVIOR:

BIGGEST OFFENDER:

FIRST TIME YOUR PARENTS HUMILIATED YOU

WHAT HAPPENED?

HOW DID YOU RESPOND?

FIRST INSECURITY:

FIRST TIME YOU FAILED AT SOMETHING

WHAT WAS IT?

WHAT WAS THE OUTCOME?

FIRST EXPOSURE TO RELIGION:

FIRST SPIRITUAL EXPERIENCE:

FIRST NEAR-DEATH EXPERIENCE

WHAT HAPPENED?

HOW WERE YOU RESCUED?

FIRST FEELING OF PRIDE:

FIRST POLITICAL ACT:

FIRST CHILDHOOD MYTH TO BE DISPELLED

MYTH:

HOW DID IT HAPPEN?

HOW DID YOU FEEL?

FIRST FAMILY CRISIS:

FIRST ENCOUNTER WITH DISCRIMINATION:

FIRST TIME YOU FELT REJECTED:

FIRST TIME YOU FELT GUILTY:

FIRST TIME YOU GOT LOST

CIRCUMSTANCES:

HOW DID YOU FIND YOUR WAY BACK?

FIRST NATURAL DISASTER YOU EXPERIENCED

WHAT WAS IT?

WHERE WERE YOU?

HOW DID YOU REACT?

FIRST TIME YOU FELT LIKE A GROWN-UP:

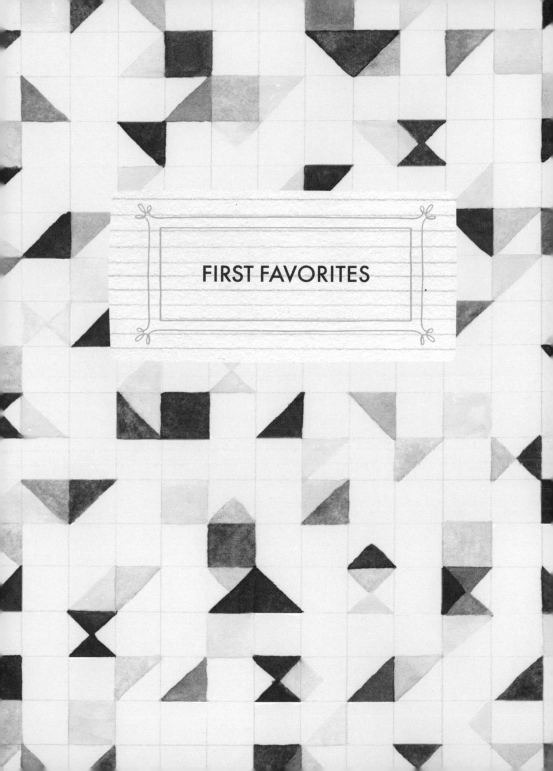

FIRST FAVORITES

FIRST FAVORITE COLOR:

FIRST FAVORITE BEDTIME STORY

TITLE:

WHO WOULD USUALLY READ IT?

FIRST FAVORITE AUTHOR:

FIRST FAVORITE BOOK

TITLE:

FIRST FAVORITE PICTURE BOOK:

FIRST FAVORITE CHAPTER BOOK:

FIRST FAVORITE MOVIE:

FIRST FAVORITE CARTOON:

FIRST FAVORITE TV SHOW

NAME:

FAVORITE CHARACTER:

FAVORITE EPISODE:

FIRST FAVORITE FOOD

FOOD:

HOW OFTEN WOULD YOU EAT IT?

FIRST FAVORITE HOLIDAY

HOLIDAY:

REASONS WHY:

FIRST TRADITIONS:

FIRST FAVORITE RELATIVE:

FIRST FAVORITE OUTFIT

COMPONENTS:

FIRST FAVORITE ARTICLE OF CLOTHING:

FIRST FAVORITE SPORT

SPORT:

WERE YOU A FAN OR PARTICIPANT?

FAVORITE PROFESSIONAL PLAYER:

FIRST FAVORITE SCHOOL SUBJECT

SUBJECT:

BEST ASSIGNMENT YOU HAD TO DO:

FIRST FAVORITE BAND

NAME:

MEMBERS:

DID YOU SEE THEM PLAY LIVE?

DID YOU OWN ANY FAN GEAR?

FIRST FAVORITE RESTAURANT

NAME:

WHAT WOULD YOU ORDER?

FIRST FAVORITE WEBSITE:

FIRST FAVORITE POSSESSION:

FIRST FAVORITE JUNK FOODS

ICE CREAM FLAVOR:

SODA:

BREAKFAST CEREAL:

PIZZA TOPPING:

FAST FOOD:

SNACK FOOD:

FIRST FAVORITE GAMES

PLAYGROUND GAME:

BOARD GAME:

FIRST FAVORITE EXTRACURRICULAR ACTIVITY:

FIRST FAVORITE ARTWORK:

FIRST MISBEHAVIORS

FIRST TIME AN ADULT OTHER THAN
YOUR PARENT SCOLDED YOU:

FIRST TIME YOU SNOOPED IN SOMEONE ELSE'S STUFF

CIRCUMSTANCES:

WHAT DID YOU FIND?

FIRST TIME YOU DISAPPOINTED YOUR PARENTS:

FIRST TIME YOU TOLD A LIE

AGE:

LIE:

TO WHO?

WHY?

WHAT WAS THE OUTCOME?

FIRST TIME YOU STOLE SOMETHING

STOLEN ITEM:

WHERE DID YOU STASH IT?

DID YOU GET CAUGHT?

FIRST TIME YOU WERE GROUNDED

REASON:

LENGTH:

FIRST PRACTICAL JOKE OR PRANK YOU PULLED

DESCRIPTION:

FIRST PRANK PULLED ON YOU:

FIRST TIME YOU BROKE SOMETHING VALUABLE

OBJECT:

ESTIMATED WORTH:

WHAT WERE THE CONSEQUENCES?

FIRST PERSON YOU ACCIDENTALLY SAW NAKED

NAME:

WHERE WERE YOU?

HOW DID THEY REACT?

FIRST PERSON WHO ACCIDENTALLY SAW YOU NAKED

NAME:

WHERE WERE YOU?

HOW DID THEY REACT?

FIRST TIME YOU HEARD ABOUT SEX

CIRCUMSTANCES:

FIRST GROWN-UP TO GIVE YOU "THE TALK":

FIRST R-RATED MOVIE YOU SAW

FIRST X-RATED MOVIE YOU SAW

FIRST TIME YOU FAKED BEING SICK

AGE:

REASONS FOR FAKING:

WHAT WERE YOUR SYMPTOMS?

DID YOU GET CAUGHT?

DID YOU TRY IT AGAIN?

FIRST PERSON TO BULLY YOU

NAME:

HOW OLD WERE YOU?

FIRST CURSE WORD

WORD:

DID YOU GET IN TROUBLE FOR SAYING IT?

WHERE DID YOU LEARN IT?

FIRST TIME YOU SAID "I HATE YOU" TO YOUR PARENTS

CIRCUMSTANCES:

HOW DID THEY RESPOND?

FIRST MUSIC YOU HID FROM YOUR PARENTS

ARTIST/BAND:

ALBUM:

FORMAT:

OFFENSIVE MATERIAL:

FIRST FISTFIGHT

OPPONENT:

REASON:

CONSEQUENCES:

FIRST TIME YOU FLUNKED A TEST

GRADE:

SUBJECT:

TEACHER:

FIRST TIME YOU CHEATED IN SCHOOL

AGE:

CHEATING METHOD:

GRADE:

DID YOU GET CAUGHT?

FIRST TIME YOU FORGED A SIGNATURE

DOCUMENT:

REASON FOR FORGERY:

DID IT WORK?

FIRST TIME YOU GOT IN TROUBLE AT SCHOOL

WHAT HAPPENED?

WHO CAUGHT YOU?

WHAT WAS YOUR PUNISHMENT?

HOW DID YOUR PARENTS REACT?

FIRST TRIP TO THE PRINCIPAL'S OFFICE:

FIRST TIME YOU CUT CLASS

GRADE:

REASONS FOR CUTTING:

WHO WAS WITH YOU?

DID YOU GET CAUGHT?

FIRST TIME YOU SNEAKED OUT OF YOUR HOUSE

AGE:

REASON FOR SNEAKING OUT:

HOW DID YOU DO IT?

DID YOU GET CAUGHT?

FIRST TIME YOU SNEAKED INTO SOMETHING

AGE:

WHY DID YOU HAVE TO SNEAK IN?

DID YOU GET CAUGHT?

FIRST VICE:

FIRST TIME YOU HAD A
SIP OF BOOZE

BEVERAGE:

LOCATION:

WHO GAVE IT TO YOU?

DID YOU LIKE IT?

FIRST TIME YOU SNEAKED OUT OF TOWN

AGE:

WHERE DID YOU GO?

WHO ELSE WAS WITH YOU?

FIRST SECRET STASH SPOT

LOCATION:

WHAT YOU STASHED THERE:

DID ANYONE EVER DISCOVER IT?

FIRST GLIMPSE OF PORNOGRAPHY

WHAT WAS IT?

WHERE WERE YOU?

WHOSE WAS IT?

FIRST CODE WORD FOR SOMETHING ILLICIT

WORD:

WHAT DID IT REFER TO?

WHO MADE IT UP?

FIRST HOUSE PARTY ATTENDED

LOCATION:

DID IT GET BUSTED?

FIRST HOUSE PARTY THAT YOU HOSTED:

FIRST TIME YOU COVERED FOR SOMEONE

CIRCUMSTANCES:

HOW DID YOU DO IT?

FIRST PIECE OF CONTRABAND DISCOVERED BY YOUR PARENTS

OFFENDING OBJECT:

WHERE WAS IT DISCOVERED?

DID YOU GET IN TROUBLE?

FIRST FRIEND DUBBED A "BAD INFLUENCE"

NAME:

REASONS:

FIRST ENCOUNTER WITH A DANGEROUS WEAPON:

FIRST RUN-IN WITH THE LAW

WHAT HAPPENED?

WHAT WERE THE CONSEQUENCES?

FIRST ACT OF VANDALISM

WHAT HAPPENED?

DID YOU GET CAUGHT?

FIRST SKINNY-DIP

AGE:

LOCATION:

WHO ELSE WAS THERE?

WERE YOU EMBARRASSED?

FIRST TATTOO

DESCRIPTION:

LOCATION ON BODY:

HOW DID YOUR PARENTS REACT?

FIRST TIME YOU WERE FIRED

JOB:

REASON FOR FIRING:

FIRST FRIEND YOU BETRAYED

NAME:

WHAT HAPPENED?

FIRST FRIEND TO BETRAY YOU:

FIRST PROMISE YOU BROKE

PROMISE:

WHO DID YOU MAKE IT TO?

CONSEQUENCES:

FIRST TIMES

FIRST TIME YOU SPENT THE NIGHT
AWAY FROM HOME

AGE:

LOCATION:

WERE YOU HOMESICK?

FIRST TIME YOU STAYED UP ALL NIGHT

AGE: LOCATION:

WHAT DID YOU DO?

DID YOU WATCH THE SUNRISE?

FIRST TIME YOU SAW
A SHOOTING STAR

AGE:

LOCATION:

DID YOU MAKE A WISH?

FIRST TIME YOU KEPT
A BIG SECRET

AGE:

SECRET:

DID YOU EVER TELL?

FIRST TIME YOU THOUGHT YOU SAW SOMETHING MAGICAL

AGE:

WHAT HAPPENED?

HOW DID YOU EXPLAIN IT AT THE TIME?

FIRST TIME YOU SAW YOUR PARENTS ARGUE

AGE:

LOCATION:

WHAT WAS THE ARGUMENT ABOUT?

FIRST TIME YOU HAD THE WIND KNOCKED OUT OF YOU:

FIRST TIME YOU THREW UP

AGE:

LOCATION:

WHAT MADE YOU SICK?

FIRST TIME YOU WERE REALLY SICK

AGE:

ILLNESS:

DURATION:

SPECIAL TLC YOU RECEIVED:

FIRST TIME YOU VISITED SOMEONE IN THE HOSPITAL

WHO WAS IT:

WHEN:

FIRST TIME YOU WERE STUNG OR BIT BY SOMETHING:

FIRST ENCOUNTER WITH A WILD ANIMAL

AGE:

LOCATION:

ANIMAL:

WHAT DID YOU DO?

HOW DID IT REACT?

FIRST TIME YOU SWAM IN A LAKE:

FIRST TIME YOU WENT FISHING

AGE: LOCATION:

WHO TOOK YOU?   DID YOU CATCH ANYTHING?

FIRST TIME YOU JUMPED OFF THE HIGH DIVE

AGE:

LOCATION:

HOW LONG DID IT TAKE FOR YOU TO WORK UP THE NERVE?

DID YOU BELLY FLOP?

FIRST TIME YOU SAW SNOW

AGE:

LOCATION:

FIRST TIME YOU BUILT A SNOWMAN:

FIRST SNOWBALL FIGHT:

FIRST TIME YOU WENT SLEDDING:

FIRST TIME YOU WENT SKIING:

FIRST TIME YOU SAW THE OCEAN

AGE: LOCATION:

DID YOU GO SWIMMING?   FIRST TIME YOU WENT SNORKELING:

FIRST TIME YOU WENT SCUBA DIVING:

FIRST HOLIDAY YOU SPENT AWAY FROM YOUR FAMILY

AGE: HOLIDAY:

WHERE WERE YOU?   HOW DID YOU CELEBRATE?

WHO ELSE WAS THERE?

FIRST TIME AT A DRIVE-IN MOVIE

AGE:

LOCATION:

WHAT MOVIE DID YOU SEE?

FIRST TIME YOU SANG KARAOKE

AGE:

LOCATION:

SONG:

FIRST TIME YOU WENT TO A PROFESSIONAL SPORTS GAME

AGE:

WHO TOOK YOU?

WHO WON?

FIRST TIME YOU WON A TROPHY:

FIRST TIME YOU FLEW IN A PLANE

AGE:

WHERE WERE YOU GOING?

HOW DID YOU FEEL?

DID YOU GET SICK?

FIRST TIME ON A TRAIN

AGE:

WHERE WERE YOU GOING?

HOW DID YOU FEEL?

DID YOU GET MOTION SICK?

FIRST TIME ON A BOAT

AGE:

WHERE WERE YOU GOING?

HOW DID YOU FEEL?

DID YOU GET SEASICK?

FIRST TIME ON A ROLLER COASTER

AGE:

LOCATION:

WERE YOU SCARED?

DID YOU GET SICK?

FIRST TIME YOU RODE A HORSE:

FIRST TIME YOU RODE A MOTORCYCLE OR SCOOTER:

FIRST CONCERT

WHO PLAYED?

AGE:

LOCATION:

WHO WENT WITH YOU?

FIRST TIME YOU DYED YOUR HAIR

AGE:

COLOR:

REACTION FROM PARENTS:

FIRST TIME YOU WERE MENTIONED IN THE NEWSPAPER

AGE:

NAME OF THE PAPER:

WHAT WAS THE ARTICLE ABOUT?

FIRST TIME YOU WERE ON TELEVISION

AGE:

WHAT WAS IT FOR?

FIRST TIME YOU PERFORMED ON STAGE

AGE:

LOCATION:

ROLE:

WHO CAME TO WATCH YOU?

FIRST TIME YOU SPOKE IN PUBLIC:

FIRST TIME YOU MADE A BIG LIFE DECISION

AGE:

DECISION:

WHAT WAS THE OUTCOME?

FIRST TIME YOU PLANTED A GARDEN

AGE:

LOCATION:

WHAT DID YOU GROW?

HOW DID IT TURN OUT?

FIRST TIME SOMEONE GAVE YOU FLOWERS

OCCASION:

TYPE OF FLOWERS:

FIRST TIME YOU QUIT A JOB

AGE:

JOB:

REASON(S) FOR QUITTING:

FIRST TIME YOU PAID A BILL

AGE:

WHAT WAS IT FOR?

AMOUNT PAID:

FIRST FUND-RAISER

CAUSE:

AMOUNT RAISED:

WHO DID YOU ASK?

FIRST TIME YOU COOKED DINNER FOR SOMEONE

AGE:

FOR WHO?

LOCATION:

MENU:

REASON FOR COOKING:

DID THEY LIKE IT?

FIRST PLACES

FIRST HOME

ADDRESS:

PHONE NUMBER:

FIRST NEXT-DOOR NEIGHBORS:

FIRST BEDROOM

COLOR:

FIRST THING YOU HUNG UP ON THE WALL:

NOTABLE DECOR:

FIRST FORT OR CLUBHOUSE

BUILDING MATERIALS:

LOCATION:

WHO COULD ENTER?

FIRST SECRET HIDING PLACE

LOCATION:

DID YOU EVER BRING ANYONE ELSE THERE?

FIRST SCHOOL

NAME:

LOCATION:

WHAT DID YOUR FIRST CLASSROOM LOOK LIKE?

BEST MEMORY:

SCHOOL MASCOT:

FIRST FAMILY VACATION

DESTINATION:

FAVORITE TRAVEL GAMES:

BEST MEMORY:

WORST MEMORY:

FIRST TRIP TO YOUR GRANDPARENTS' HOUSE

LOCATION:

WHAT DO YOU REMEMBER MOST ABOUT THEIR HOUSE?

FIRST FAMILY REUNION

LOCATION:

WHICH FAMILY MEMBERS DID YOU MEET FOR THE FIRST TIME?

FIRST TRIP TO THE ZOO

LOCATION:

AGE:

WHAT ANIMAL WAS YOUR FAVORITE?

FIRST CAMPING TRIP

LOCATION:

WHO WENT?

FIRST SUMMER CAMP

NAME:

CAMP FRIENDS:

BEST MEMORY:

FIRST AMUSEMENT PARK

NAME:

LOCATION:

WHAT WAS YOUR FAVORITE RIDE?

WHAT DID YOU EAT?

FIRST WATER PARK

NAME:

LOCATION:

WHAT WAS YOUR FAVORITE ATTRACTION?

FIRST HAUNTED HOUSE

LOCATION:

WHAT SCARED YOU THE MOST?

FIRST FAMOUS LANDMARK YOU VISITED:

FIRST SCHOOL TRIP

DESTINATION:

GRADE:

BEST MEMORY:

FIRST TRIP TO A FARM

LOCATION:

WHAT DO YOU REMEMBER
SEEING THERE?

FIRST TRIP TO A MUSEUM

NAME:

LOCATION:

WHAT DO YOU REMEMBER
SEEING THERE?

FIRST HOTEL YOU REMEMBER STAYING IN

NAME:

LOCATION:

FIRST TIME YOU STAYED ALONE IN A HOTEL:

FIRST BANK

NAME:

FIRST DEPOSIT AMOUNT:

FIRST OVERDRAFT:

FIRST FAVORITE CLOTHING STORE

NAME:

LOCATION:

WHAT WOULD YOU LOOK FOR THERE?

FIRST FAVORITE COFFEE SHOP

NAME:

LOCATION:

WHAT WOULD YOU ORDER?

FIRST HANGOUT SPOT

NAME:

LOCATION:

WHO HUNG OUT THERE?

FIRST MUSIC FESTIVAL

FESTIVAL NAME:

LOCATION:

WHO PLAYED?

BEST MEMORY:

FIRST DORM ROOM

BUILDING NAME:

ROOM NUMBER:

ROOMMATE(S):

NOTABLE ROOM DECOR:

FIRST ROAD TRIP WITH FRIENDS

DESTINATION:

FELLOW TRAVELERS:

WHAT MUSIC DID YOU LISTEN TO?

FIRST COLLEGE COURSE

TITLE OF COURSE:

BEST THING YOU LEARNED IN THE CLASS:

FIRST TRIP TO A FOREIGN COUNTRY

COUNTRY:

AGE:

BIGGEST DIFFERENCE YOU NOTICED:

BEST MEMORY:

FIRST WEDDING YOU ATTENDED

LOCATION:

COUPLE'S NAMES:

FIRST APARTMENT

ADDRESS:

RENT:

ROOMMATES:

BEST THING ABOUT THE APARTMENT:

WORST THING ABOUT THE APARTMENT:

LANDLORD:

REASON FOR LEAVING:

TENURE:

FONDEST MEMORY:

FIRST CONNECTIONS

YOUR VERY FIRST FRIEND

NAME:

WHERE ARE THEY NOW?.

FIRST BEST FRIEND

NAME:

WHEN DID YOU BECOME FRIENDS?

HOW DID YOU MEET?

FIRST PEN PAL

NAME:

WHERE DID THEY LIVE?

HOW DID YOU START WRITING?

DID YOU EVER MEET IN PERSON?

FIRST FRENEMY

NAME:

GOOD QUALITIES:

BAD QUALITIES:

FIRST ENEMY

NAME:

REASON YOU WERE ENEMIES:

DID YOU EVER BECOME FRIENDS?

FIRST BLOWOUT FIGHT
WITH A FRIEND

FRIEND'S NAME:

REASON FOR FIGHT:

DID YOU EVER MAKE UP?

FIRST CLIQUE

MEMBERS:

HOW WOULD YOU HAVE
DESCRIBED YOURSELVES?

FIRST FRIEND TO MOVE AWAY

NAME:

WHERE DID THEY MOVE?

FIRST BABYSITTER

NAME:

MOST MEMORABLE THINGS YOU DID WITH YOUR BABYSITTER:

DID THEY LET YOU DO ANYTHING YOUR PARENTS WOULDN'T?

FIRST TIME YOU BABYSAT SOMEONE ELSE

WHO DID YOU BABYSIT?

SALARY:

FIRST TEACHER

NAME:

FIRST TEACHER YOU HATED:

FIRST TEACHER YOU LOVED:

FIRST MENTOR

NAME:

MOST VALUABLE LESSON THEY TAUGHT YOU:

FIRST FRIEND TO GET MARRIED:

FIRST FRIEND TO GET PREGNANT

NAME:

HOW DID YOU FIND OUT?

WHAT HAPPENED?

FIRST FASHION IDOL

NAME:

STYLE ELEMENTS YOU ADOPTED:

FIRST FAMOUS PERSON YOU MET

NAME:

LOCATION:

WHAT WERE THEY LIKE?

FIRST PRESIDENT YOU REMEMBER

NAME:

FIRST PERSON YOU VOTED FOR:

WHO WERE THEIR OPPONENTS?

FIRST FRIEND TO
BECOME FAMOUS

NAME:

WHAT WERE THEY FAMOUS FOR?

FIRST FRIEND TO
BECOME INFAMOUS

NAME:

WHAT WERE THEY INFAMOUS FOR?

FIRST LOVES AND
RELATIONSHIPS

FIRST CRUSH

NAME:

FIRST CELEBRITY CRUSH:

FIRST CRUSH ON
AN OLDER PERSON:

FIRST SLOW DANCE

DANCE PARTNER:

LOCATION:

SONG:

FIRST LOVE

NAME:

HOW YOU MET:

FIRST KISS

PARTNER:

AGE:

LOCATION:

FIRST DATE

NAME OF DATE:

WHAT YOU DID:

DID YOU KISS?

FIRST ROMANTIC DINNER

DINNER COMPANION:

LOCATION:

WHAT YOU ATE:

WHO PAID:

FIRST PERSON WHO WROTE YOU A LOVE LETTER

NAME:

WHERE YOU MET:

DID YOU WRITE THEM BACK?

FIRST PERSON YOU THOUGHT YOU WOULD MARRY

NAME:

WHERE ARE THEY NOW?

FIRST TIME YOU FOOLED AROUND

PARTNER:

HOW OLD WERE YOU?

WHERE WERE YOU?

FIRST MAKE-OUT SPOT

LOCATION:

DID YOU EVER GET CAUGHT MAKING OUT THERE?

FIRST TIME YOU SPENT THE NIGHT WITH SOMEONE

NAME:

LOCATION:

DID YOUR PARENTS FIND OUT?

FIRST TIME YOU SAID "I LOVE YOU"

TO WHO?

HOW OLD WERE YOU?

WHERE WERE YOU?

HOW DID THEY REACT?

FIRST PARTNER YOUR PARENTS DIDN'T APPROVE OF

NAME:

REASONS FOR DISAPPROVAL:

FIRST SONG YOU SHARED WITH SOMEONE

SONG:

WHO DID YOU SHARE IT WITH?

HOW DID IT BECOME YOUR SONG?

FIRST TIME SOMEONE TOLD YOU THEY LOVED YOU

WHO WAS IT?

HOW DID YOU RESPOND?

FIRST SECRET ADMIRER

NAME USED:

HOW THEY CONTACTED YOU:

DID YOU EVER DISCOVER
THEIR TRUE IDENTITY?

FIRST PERSON WHO
BROKE YOUR HEART

NAME:

FIRST PERSON WHOSE HEART
YOU BROKE:

FIRST BIG COUPLE'S FIGHT

NAME OF PARTNER:

REASON FOR FIGHT:

DID IT CAUSE YOU TO BREAK UP?

FIRST FIT OF ROMANTIC JEALOUSY

CIRCUMSTANCES:

HOW DID YOU REACT?

HOW DID YOUR PARTNER REACT?

FIRST PET NAME GIVEN TO YOU

NAME:

FIRST PET NAME YOU CALLED SOMEONE ELSE:

FIRST PERSON YOU CHEATED ON

NAME:

WHO DID YOU CHEAT WITH?

DID YOUR PARTNER EVER FIND OUT?

FIRST PERSON TO CHEAT ON YOU

NAME:

HOW DID YOU FIND OUT?

FIRST ONE-NIGHT STAND

NAME:

DID YOU REGRET IT?

DID YOU EVER SEE THEM AGAIN?

FIRST FLING

NAME:

HOW LONG DID IT LAST?

FIRST NEW YEAR'S EVE KISS

NAME OF KISSER:

YEAR:

ISBN: 978-1-4521-1830-7

Manufactured in China

MIX
Paper from
responsible sources
FSC® C008047

Designed by Kayla Ferriera
Text by Lucien Edwards
Illustrations by Amy Borrell

10 9 8 7 6 5 4 3 2

Chronicle Books LLC
680 Second Street
San Francisco, California 94107
www.chroniclebooks.com